MW01231801

TOTALLY BOGUS MEN II

Social Guide for Younger American Women

to Chelsea ☺

Chip Bunce and Tony Lolas, Ph.D.

Bunce, Chip Gregory Alan
Lolas, Anthony Joseph

Totally Bogus Men II: Social Guide for Younger American Women

Published in Atlanta, Georgia

First published by Dog Ear Publishing
4010 W. 86th Street, Ste H
Indianapolis, IN 46268
www.dogearpublishing.net

ISBN: 978-159858-632-9

This book is printed on acid-free paper.

Printed in the United States of America

DEDICATION

This book is dedicated to the women who have learned to go for quality, versus quantity, in their individual pursuit of finding "Mister Right."

ACKNOWLEDGEMENTS

We are most grateful for the younger men who have chosen to set the example, taking the "higher path" of life rather than succumbing to pressure to "fit in" with the demented masses of baggy-pant-wearing, under-wear-displaying, backward-baseball-cap-sporting, ear-ring-infested, tattoo-riddled buffoons. It will be interesting to see how many men will be dressing and acting this way when they are 40 years old.

Special thanks to Stephanie for her generosity with costumes and props from her Atlanta store *Psycho Sisters Consignment,* 5964 Roswell Road.

TABLE OF CONTENTS

FOREWORD

The circumstances and people described in this book are designed to provoke thought and provide entertainment. When looking at ourselves and others, we should be willing to laugh at the things that make life interesting.

Although this book is oriented toward the "Younger American Woman," there are many passages that should be shared with the men in their lives.

Before there can be change, one must be aware of the need for change. Consequently, this book can be an opportunity to open dialogue with your significant other.

So grab a glass of wine or juice, sit back, and enjoy the ride!

WHO ARE
"YOUNGER AMERICAN WOMEN"?

Our first answer is that younger American women are obviously older than *zero*, but younger than *one hundred*. To be more exact, and knowing that all women would love to be included in the *YOUNG* category, we had to set the limit from age 18 to 39, regardless whether you're single, recently single, unmarried, marriage annulled, divorced, separated, thinking about getting separated, have children, no children, and every other category we are probably missing. The good news is, if you are a woman reading this and you have already bought this book, you are awarded the meritorious *YOUNG* designation for today! Congratulations on joining the newest ranks of quality American women who are ready for Mister Right.

If you are an American woman *OVER* the age of one hundred, you get highest honors!

Patiently waiting for Mister Right

INTERVIEW WITH
DAPHNE THE VAMPIRE

Finding *hidden* bogus men is a formidable task, as many operate by stealth and emerge only when they can prey upon an unsuspecting woman.

To accomplish this objective, we hired *Daphne* to go undercover. Daphne was never afraid to reach all levels of clandestine work, while being careful not to go literally *under the covers.*

Here's a short interview recap of her success:

Tony: Welcome back, Daphne and thank you for taking time in the FIELD!

Daphne: Thanks Tony, it was a lot of fun! By dressing the part, it helped set the tone, so to speak, and bring out perhaps the entire spectrum of hidden bogus men from all walks of life.

Chip: Hi Daphne! Taking on such an important mission will be a tribute to single women all across America. Please tell us how you helped prepare for such a mission!

Daphne: Thanks, Chip. By preparing, I had to put my mind into the sick, psychotic world of totally bogus men. Going GOTHIC was the key.

Tony: When you say "Going gothic," what does that mean?

Daphne: It means that I had to find the right clothes for the right atmosphere. I had to visualize how twisted many American men are, and get into that frame of mind. And more importantly, I had to think what would magnetically pull them over to me.

Chip: What was your toughest challenge?

Daphne: Outside colleges and universities. I figured the short skirt with the flashy black top would bring in some of these bad boys in the parking lot. And it worked! The bogus men came in like flies, asking me out on a date, trying to get my number, and in one case, a bogus man tried following me home!

Tony: Followed you home! That's incredible. How did you handle that?

Daphne: The latch on my trunk never did work well, and when I opened the trunk while being followed, the fertilizer flew out, hit his windshield, and the next thing you know, he hit a tree. You could say the @@@@ really hit the fan!

Chip: What bogus man experience is your personal favorite?

Daphne: Great question! I think going undercover in many high class lounges and bars. So many of these guys pretended being a *geographical bachelor.* Either it was married men who were suddenly *single,* or single men who seemed desperate to *get married.*

Tony: Geographical bachelor! I like it! Can you go into further detail?

Daphne: Would love to! Wearing gothic black brings out the most mysterious of bogus men. Usually married, but careful to conceal, these slight of hand experts are quick to remove their wedding ring, leaving only the tiny, almost unnoticeable tan line on their left finger. The guy who approached me was no lightweight.

Acting with a style of sophistication and later throwing out time-tested words of promised love, I could see how so many women would fall for such drama. Are they sensing something capable, or promising, in his manner? His eyes alone provided years of intense study. Unbeknown to me at the time, here was a true master at the art of romantic deception.

Going GOTHIC felt curiously good !

The RED miniskirt was IDEAL for the college parking lot

Spike, the DOG, let me borrow his collar

Sometimes, Going GOTHIC, requires being in the PINK

Mini MO was always ready to lend a HAND

Going Gothic was dark and mysterious

A good Vampire Girl always finds the bar

"They call me Rodney," he muttered, eagerly admiring my lips and figure in black.

"What do you do, Rodney?" I responded.

Apparently he wasn't quite ready for such a round of questions, and thinking of something to say, he answered, "Fighter pilot, Air Force."

Pretending to be impressed, I offered, "Wow, a real war hero! What do you fly?"

"They call me Top Gun back at the base. I fly the F14 Tomcat. It's got that swing wing design."

"Swing wing, hey?" F14, Air Force, brought out the warning sign! The only thing swingin' about this bogus man was hidden in his trousers, and I didn't want to take out my magnifying glass.

Rodney continued, "What do you say we take off, and I'll show you the evening sky? We can go up, up and away."

"Not quite ready to go up with you, Rodney. There aren't any F14's in the Air Force. Next time, make sure you do your research on Air Force jets!"

Tony: Pretty wild! I was a fighter pilot in the Air Force; and you're right, those are Navy jets. F15 or F16 would have been a better selection.

Daphne: You are right! Rodney was such a bogus man! Fortunately, he was easy to spot.

Chip: Did you find yourself going to dark, underground clubs too?

Daphne: I did, and that also was quite bizarre. Besides the music, and weird lights, I found it claustrophobic. Many men in the vampire underground would gang up and surround me, giving me the feeling of being trapped and closed in. I felt like a victim as they circled me looking for the kill!

Tony: What did you do?

Daphne: I needed help, and called *MINI MO*, my assistant, to help get me out! Only 3 feet tall, Mini can easily slip under people's legs, around tight spots, and even under furniture, radioing for help or preparing an escape plan. I'd be stuck in many sticky situations had it not been for *MINI MO* (photo attached).

Chip: You are fortunate for anticipating the need for *MINI MO.* Quite an accomplishment, Daphne! Tony and I thank you for your unselfish service in helping women all across the country.

Tony: Thank you, Daphne! We'll most likely have more classified Bogus man missions for you down the road!

Daphne: 24 / 7! You have my cell phone. You guys are GREAT!

Thank you for the opportunity to expose the Bogus Men whom I have experienced to my sisters!! By exposing the full range of behaviors by Bogus Men, I'm hoping we can change their behavior, and make the world a better place for both men and women.

YOUNGER WOMEN'S INTRODUCTORY COURSE IN FINDING MISTER RIGHT

"The least of things with a meaning is worth more in life than the greatest of things without it."

Carl Jung (1875 – 1961)

As with so many things in life, a woman comes to realize that quality offers substantially more value to her well-being than quantity. A woman can purchase 100 pairs of shoes, but the one pair that offers elegance, style, comfort, and appeal certainly is her most treasured. Take a look at jewelry; she may own earrings, bracelets, and necklaces for every occasion, but her most treasured possession is often the wedding ring.

Did you just call me BI POLAR ?

Finding Mister Right can be no different than shopping for shoes or jewelry. There are literally TONS of guys out there. If you don't believe that, just take a tour at one of the PRISONS.

Going online with a venti mocha in hand, today's ambitious, single woman has the worldwide range of the Internet at her disposal, from the simple E-Har-MAN-HE dot com to BI-SPACE dot com to every other woman's single's ad: "I want a guy to sit back with, watch a movie, and chill—maybe taking romantic walks on the beach."

How bout a double date with me and Leroy ?

Too much technology. Too much click and send. Not enough quality. Not enough true meaning. Not enough trust!

So where does today's active woman go? Now that's a good one.

Hell if we know. But it seems that going somewhere to find this most intriguing Mister Right isn't as important as recognizing the Mister Right, or Mister Wrong, qualities BEFORE he starts trying to peel off your panties. No sense in getting a *positive* on the home pregnancy test only to find this guy is on probation for armed robbery. Unless, of course, there is a Bonnie and CLYDE vacancy on the job-bank website.

Think back to all the really botched up men you've dated so far. That's right, all the way BACK. Don't be ashamed. At first, it was cute to date the high school JOCK boy, who was all set for the NFL until he got arrested for selling crystal meth in the school parking lot on Saturday night. Or what about your BAD BOY, you know, the guy with a ride JOHN DEARE wouldn't dare manufacture—a cross between an antiterrorist combat assault vehicle and a Moonraker. Music so loud, the pest control business would go OUT of business. Not even a cockroach can stand Rappy Dappy without long-term sinus and ear canal damage.

What about your ole fraternit-HE boy, Sigma Zippie Yippie Alpha Eat Pie Omega Delta Forest Jean Claude Van Diesel college-girls-gawn-wild PARTEE BOY? What about the smelly, earwax-infested, not-enough-toilet-paper and don't use much soap after the bad room greeze monkee COWBOY? What about tough boy militar-HE chewin-tobacco-spittin, rippin, ain't he hippin, SOLDIER BOY who hasn't bothered in months to ask, "How was your day?" while he's checkin out the babe at the drive thru? What about sleepin' with the enem-HE YUPPIE BOY with mobile phone in hand, who cares more about what imaginary guys you are sleepin' with while he's got little black book volumes one and two?

Yes, chances are you've seen all that crap and more while pretty much dating every Mister Wrong on the planet. So sit up and enjoy a ride on the wild side— A woman's eternal search for Mister Right. It's time you shake things up. Big! Take our advice: the best way to find Mr. Right is to learn to steer clear of this catalogue of Mr. Wrongs. Here's a field guide to Bogus Men to avoid, to help you find Lasting Love!

UNDERWEAR-STICKING-OUT BAGGY MAN

Our mothers took particular pride in keeping our FROOT of the LUME underwear in proper stock. To us, it was one of the best ways to start the day. The sheer joy of pulling them on after a refreshing shower! Wearing clean jockey underpants was a hidden secret to feeling good all over. And being a secret, it felt important to keep underpants properly covered. Why should other friends and schoolmates know these innermost practices? Keeping it a secret from other men is especially important since some of us like to wear different colors depending on our mood.

Mothers of today's male youth may not have benefited from the same underwear training as our Moms. What else could account for the ubiquitous display of baggy pants and underwear that seem predisposed to the outside environment? But even if a mother fails to show her 4-year-old son the value of keeping his underpants hidden, what's to keep him, at age 20, from pulling his outer pants back up?

Today's immature DUDE not only accepts baggy pants as standard uniform issue, but looks with disdain on men who choose to utilize a belt. What could cause

Nothi' quite like a sharp dressed man

this silly display? Could it be a sense of compassion? After all, if we were cooped up like fresh underwear in a plastic wrapping for weeks or months, we would welcome the opportunity to get a whiff of the outside. No telling how long some of that underwear has been holding its breath, just waiting for the day that someone would purchase it and tear open that three-pack. Ahh, the relief!

We've also researched whether there might be a literal shortage of men's belts in department and clothing stores. No such luck. It seems just about everywhere, there were hundreds of belts waiting for selection.

Then we had to think even deeper. Could it be a treatment program for underwear, which, having gained not much attention over the years, would be in need of greater self-confidence? Perhaps exposing today's male underwear to the rigors of the outdoors, including the variations in temperature, humidity, and rough surfaces, will pave the way for an even stronger, more versatile generation of younger underpants to come. After all, who would be proud of wearing a wimpy, milquetoast pair of jockey shorts? By the way, I still don't know why they call it a *pair* or jockey shorts when I only wear one.

And, there are literally hundreds of different colors from which to choose! Here we thought that underwear only came in white. Not true. And avoid the headache of just adding color. Put some SPICE into it! Today's baggy-pant male can display goldfish, frogs, pink hearts, seashells, smiley-faces, hotdogs, construction tools, drill bits, hammers, screwdrivers, wrenches, nuts, bolts, staplers, chewing tobacco, bubble gum, red roses, yellow roses, blue roses, thorny roses, baseballs, footballs, soccer balls, basketballs, softballs, tennis

The FUTURE of the American male. Good luck

balls, ping pong balls, rubber hoses, chewin' tobacco cans, distributors, clutches, gear box ratios, garden hoses, nozzles, pictures of the beach, sandcastles, college diplomas, mathematic formulas, answers to last week's physics exam, the entire chemistry periodic table, halogens, and noble gases. Well, the gases might not be so noble; it depends on the quantity of beans he ate the night before.

The interesting fact is, no matter where we go, we cannot escape advertising. Billboards, television commercials, bumper stickers, and yes, even men who wear baggy pants, all convey an initial image, impression, or idea that signals a style, a trend, an attitude. A baggy-underpants male is simply advertising to the world what a total IDIOT he truly is.

Looking ahead, and taking gravity into the equation, does it not stand to reason that, in time, men will not bother with any outer clothing at all? Why limit only part of the male underwear to the environment? It would make sense, in the interest of diversity, to allow all the fabric—front, sides, elastic band at the top—to be fully free to experience life to the fullest. Once men get the idea that it's totally acceptable to walk around in underwear alone, imagine the cost savings in wardrobes. Even simple tasks, like utilizing men's urinals, make for quicker operations while simultaneously saving more time during the busy day. No need to unzip anything—which means *shorter lines* in the men's room. All men can join in on the fun! Start underwear parties in the men's room; order in some pizza and cold beer. With the toilet within reach, it's a win-win package. It could be such fun to spend the entire weekend in the men's restroom.

Try walking to the kitchen with your pants down to your knees, and you'd fall over on the way to the coffeepot. Could it be a similar skill to skateboarding, where a certain level of dexterity, balance, and momentum must be learned before more substantial tasks like climbing up stairs is attempted? In time, those better qualified professionals can then go on to the *OLYMPICS* of jogging, running, and mountaineering, where the knees and hips must work in tandem to reach higher elevations or avoid road obstacles. Imagine earning the gold medal in baggy-pant climbing!

When we see men wearing their pants down to the *BAGGY* position, it is tempting to call 9-1-1. Could these be patients who mistakenly missed their antidepressant medication? Are they signaling to local police, EMT, and medical personnel to help in their quest for assistance? Wearing baggy pants *half mast* exposes a brain *half full*!

Because today's astute woman can recognize the danger signs of the *BAGGY PANT MAN* 40 or 50 feet away from initial contact, they can be grateful that these men, much like the dorsal fins of an approaching shark, are providing an early warning to *STAY CLEAR*. Those with *diarrhea* need another 50-foot clearance!

NO-ANGEL BAD BOYS

Chip once owned a *BMW R65LS* motorcycle, while stationed with the US Navy in the Republic of Panama, Panama Canal. What a great bike! Shaft drive, disc brakes, excellent torque for rapid initial acceleration, smooth shifting, comfortable seat, and even 4-way flashers and tool kit were included!

But this chapter has nothing to do with any motorcycle, motorized vehicle, or motorcycle club or organization. Rather, this chapter talks about the big bully behavior of any man who displays his tough-boy image wherever he may go—inside the shopping mall, dropping off clothes at the cleaners, and maybe taking the car to a car wash on Saturday afternoon.

Regardless of the dress or attire, these No-Angel Bad Boys never truly evolved from grade school. Even those with high school diplomas or GEE HEE DEEZE. Having graduated really means nothing to these kids. What matters most is being the bad boy on the block. Fear, intimidation, and power create a certain atmosphere that scares many men, but curiously appeals to some women, who melt like a stick of butter on the open grill.

I Be one BAD, BAD, BOY

New tires: VEESA. Tank fill up: VEESA.
Getting your hearing back? PRICELESS

But deep inside the tough-boy image, the No-Angel Bad Boy is definitely confused and lost. Not recognizing his own true personality or inner strengths, he drifts through life looking for people's reaction to his outer image, special style, or in some cases, special odor.

When does the Barbershop close tonite?

To be accurate, the first true No-Angel Bad Boy was probably Peking Man, going back several millennia, when the Gillette Track 5 shaving kit had not yet been invented. In those days, a simple trip to the Prehistoric Grocery Store or Oil Change Service Center often meant dealing with monstrous flying pterodactyls or Tyrannosaurus beasts. This is a time when few cavemen would even think about heading off to work wearing wire-rimmed glasses, toting suitcases, or dangling mobile phones (not yet invented). Back then, they had to be tough! If they weren't, those animals would have told their friends, and next thing you know, Peking Man would have been a Peking Dead Duck. *And you wouldn't be reading this!*

In prehistoric times, knowing how to act tough, and being smelly and rude not only made total sense, it was the order of the day. And not having the benefit of watching Doctor Phil on the television, Cavewomen assumed that all men were supposed to be smelly, rough and powerful, with or without their wooden clubs.

Centuries later, despite the development of the Internet and cars that run on gasoline, diesel fuel, battery, or hybrid technology, many of these same Cave Men never truly went away. In fact, neither did the smell.

But now that we're all in the 21st century (we think), it's time for men to leave some of the old styles of the past behind. Why not evolve from the campfire-building, wooden-club-toting, bearded two-legged human ape to one who takes frequent showers during the week, and uses soap, deodorant, shampoo, fingernail grooming, toenail grooming, mouthwash, etc.?

There is probably no single way to recognize a true No-Angel Bad Boy. These days many No-Angels may wear black leather attire for a Sunday drive, but could rapidly shift to coat and tie as the occasion requires. But, they keep the same aggressive style hidden on the inside. For example, a No-Angel Bad Boy may be considerate enough to open the door for someone, say, on his way to the next meth manufacturing center, or perhaps offer a cup of coffee to a fellow distributor at the annual West Coast weapons sale and

Of course I was in Special Forces.
Don't let the look fool you

arms trafficking convention.

Or, he may be just a country boy who likes to over-power anyone new at his favorite bar—ambushing the poor lad standing next to him. A No-Angel Bad Boy may find it appropriate not only to get drunk, but reach full intoxication, then create fights, mischief, or other disruption even though he probably won't feel it anyway.

Women who seem to enjoy the Primitive Man approach will never have to worry about being bored. But even if you do, the real question might be better asked, "How well can you handle 20 of his drunk friends who are coming over later tonight?"

Electroshock therapy may be one answer here. Seems to me that we've seen videos in the laboratory where lab rats and mice learned how to adjust their behavior after being subjected to a small electrical *zap*. Unlike mice or lab rats, however, today's No-Angel Bad Boy may find the *TASER* style electrical bolt more refreshing and enjoyable, restoring perhaps a lost sense of smell or taste buds long wasted on kegs of beer.

Very social creatures, No-Angel Bad Boys love to come ridin' into town, perhaps on a cow or donkey, their odor and growls saturating an otherwise quiet restaurant or bar whose only activity on a Saturday night was the juke box and pinball machine.

Time travel back to prehistoric days may allow many of today's women the opportunity to fully immerse themselves in this primitive way of life. No sense in set-tling just for the appetizer! If you're hankering for a taste of sheer brutal power, time travel may just be for you! Otherwise, recognize the symptoms!

BEE-BOP, HIPPY HOP BOY

Partying like a Rock Star may be fun and dandy, but the real question is, why not sell baseball caps that completely cover the entire person? In other words, to me it's simply incomplete to have a baseball cap backwards, sideways, cocked up 45 degrees toward the jet stream, or covering only part of your ears. No sir!

I say, go ALL THE WAY! Something that Frank Sin-HAT-ra may even have sung about. For the manufacturers out there, if I may say so, I recommend that you start making the baseball caps size XXXXXXXXXXL.

The New Hat needs to be big enough to cover a full-grown man walkin' down the street. All you should see is a giant baseball cap that seems to be *floating* just above the sidewalk.

For those Bee-Bop Hippy Hop Boys who drive automobiles, special holes in the cap may be authorized to allow for an increased field of vision, particularly important for safety, of course.

Bee-Bop Hippy Hop Boys (Bee-Bops for short) are never satisfied with a baseball cap designed for its original purpose, which probably had something to do with either (A) a *baseball*, (B) a *casual head apparel,* a device intended to keep oneself cool and unburned under bright, sunny conditions, or (C) a means for *protecting one's eyes* from the bright sun.

" Its all about da money babe "

Bee-Bop Boys, however, take the baseball cap in a whole new direction—or lack thereof. Backwards, for example, most likely means that they are going *nowhere* in their lives, and, recognizing this fact, they are asking society to help them find the spot where they went astray and maybe guide them in the right direction. Where have you NOT seen tons of backwards-baseball-cap boys across the country? You'll want to avoid them, of course. The backwards baseball cap syndrome may be induced by low self-esteem and small appendage.

Other novel approaches to baseball-hat-wearing are apparently due to a brain irregularity similar to a confused compass smashed on a deserted island that shifts *West, East, North,* or *South* on a moment's notice. Those with more creative minds may even diversify direction of their baseball cap to, say, *East by Southeast,* pointing to an inspiring Caribbean cruise with fresh cocktails along the way. Still others may choose *West by Southwest,* reminiscent of the gun-slinger days of the Old West.

Bee-Bop Boys are rarely complete without their music. You can tell them not only by the type of music they have selected, but also, and more important, is the level of volume. After interviewing professionals in the pest control business, we've learned that even bugs and crawling insects, like the infamous cockroach, don't like really loud music. Could it be that Bee-Bop Boys are in training for a new career in pest control?

To feel truly complete, a Bee-Bop Boy thoroughly enjoys driving with his windows down, displaying 24" chrome wheels, revving his engine to demonstrate his nitrous oxide conversion capability, displaying his self-initiated compass-direction baseball cap, and playing LOUD, *LOUD* music that somehow misses the attention of local police authorities on most occasions, unfortunately. Bee-Bops are so addled by the booming basslines and their pardee-time attitude that fundamental driving techniques like proper turn-signal use, ample stopping-distance from the car in front of them, or attending to traffic flow, elude them. Even walking down the sidewalk, Bee-Bop behavior announces "Get OUTTA my WAY, boy."

Give these guys a wide berth as they bop past you!

For employers looking to hire professional people for their vacancies, it would seem that a career in SECURITY would be ideal for a Bee-Bop Boy because he can completely confuse a would-be thief or burglar with his baseball cap. The LOUD music is also helpful to interrupt a burglar's communication system.

Women who cling to the Bee-Bop program may need some time away on a deserted island, with gently lapping ocean waves and an occasional seagull cawing overhead. Even the most raucous flock of seagulls in a howling typhoon will seem serene after experiencing the Bee-Bop Hippy Hop Boy. And with his confused sense of direction, he'll never find you without your help. So, don't help!!

GOOD OL' BOY
IN MY PICK-UP TRUCK

I'M A GOOD OL' BOY IN MY PICK-UP TRUCK,
MY LADY FRIENDS HAVE ALL THE LUCK.
I'M DRUNK BY TWO, THEN I GRAB ME SOME
CHEW,
C'MON, HONEY, WANNA @@@@?

Good Ol' Boys and big ol' pick-up trucks go hand
in hand. It is unlikely that today's Good Ol' Boy is driving the new Bentley convertible, the Ferrari 599, or a
Bugatti. SUV's don't really count either, since manufacturers have offered so many luxury features on today's
Sports Utility Vehicles to accommodate needy "soccer
moms." What is important to a Good Ol' Boy is to
ensure that his pick-up truck makes a statement by taking up most of the parking lot!

Good Ol' Boys love their trucks. And we ain't
talkin' about just some stock truck from the dealership.
Good Ol' Boys are ready to haul cattle, pigs, goats,
chickens, wild dogs, sheep, and bundles of dirt and hay
on a moment's notice. This requires a solid logistical
platform.

Yeah, it's BIG. Just like me.

First, Good Ol' Boys need tires that *ain't sold in regular stores*. Commercial-grade bulldozer suppliers offer a plentiful selection of mega-tires, so the vehicle's new center of gravity is raised to the level of a football goal post. And what a treat for other cars during stop-lights! Higher elevation offers a tremendous undercar-riage view of Good Ol's oil pan!

Owning a towering *PA* system is yet another hid-den benefit, as it allows the entire neighborhood to hear inane talk radio shows, sports, weather, rap, country, oldies rock, football scores, soy bean data, and even real estate commercials as the Good Ol' Boy maneuvers his vehicle for final approach. Coupled with a roaring engine and overhead searchlights, Good Ol's want you to know, Dey are comin' THRU!

Often, Good Ol's have integrated their vehicular appendage with the backwards baseball cap syndrome, signaling both misdirection and confusion as they ride your rear bumper in busy city rush hour traffic. Driving alongside a Good Ol' in traffic may be of particular con-cern should recycled chewing tobacco and spit find its way onto your windshield. Or perhaps you'll notice a new string of empty beer cans trailing in their wake, lending new meaning to signs instructing *DON'T TRASH OUR HIGHWAYS*.

What exactly are Good Ol's trying to pick up in their Pick-up truck? Are they trying to pick up women? That's got to be the underlying hidden benefit, as we've seen many women enticed by a pair of *dangling fur dice* under the front mirror. And you don't have to live in the *country* to be a Good Ol', either. Many Good Ol's have infiltrated cities and mid-sized townships across the country. Since it's important to them that they make their statement by taking up two parking spaces in traditional parking lots, it is helpful to remember that in making you walk another 200 yards to Wal-Dart, you are actually getting more exercise, thanks to this syndrome.

Should Good Ol's continue to raise the elevation these next several years, we anticipate the Federal Aviation Administration will require *AIRCRAFT WARNING LIGHTS* as incoming pick-ups approach. Add in a pair of wings and tail fins, and Good Ol' will be offering flights to Nebraska on weekends.

Before you take up with one of these boys, ladies, remember the favorite bumper sticker of the Good Ol' boy:

My wife said either my truck goes or she does.

I'll miss you, honey!

Take heed if you don't want to be second fiddle to a truck!!

EARRING LEERING—
AIN'T HE HEARING?

Starting to date in high school, one of the first things to learn was the necessity to compliment a woman on her choice in jewelry—in particular, her beautiful earrings. It seems women today have earrings for formal dinner occasions, such as discrete small diamonds or single pearls. Women wanting a bit more fashion choose larger earrings, often adding necklaces, rings, or bracelets suggesting a common theme, such as a heart which is an advertisement for love itself. The colors, naturally, are chosen to match a dress or accentuate the feminine make-up and lipstick.

We've seen jewelry in all shapes, colors, and sizes, including rings the size of Ping Pong balls. Then there's plastic; stainless steel; aluminum; chrome; 10, 12, 14, 18, 24-carat yellow gold; white gold; pink gold; silver; and in all shapes: squares, triangles, rectangles, trapezoids, dolphins, minnows, sharks; and in different stones: diamonds, pretend diamonds, turquoises, sapphires, rubies, and probably even prizes from the bubble gum machine.

I only wear the BEST in jewelry

Unless we missed it along the way, though, while growing up, we don't think we ever saw one guy wearing an earring in school, or anywhere else for that matter. To do so was to guarantee ridicule, if not a towel fight in the boy's locker room during gym class. We even remember getting snapped just for not tying shoelaces, or getting pinned!

When some of the Hollywood actors and rock musicians started wearing jewelry, it seemed odd at first, of course, but perhaps they could make the case that it was justified, considering many of them were making several million dollars a year. But then, like a floodgate, it was everywhere! Grown men, teenage boys, college

Which way to the MALL ?

students, those in graduate school, the workplace, car mechanics, construction workers, doctors, lawyers, athletes, garbage collectors, even unemployed men, found glamour in the male earring. And soon both ears were punctured in many places.

Earrings, now coupled with other facial adjustments such as nose, eyebrow, lip, and tongue piercing, have granted today's confused men parity with women's fashion, women's jewelry, and women's public image. Women shouldn't feel threatened by the competition because, with increased demand and inflation, the price of gold is going up to levels unheard of in the past. As a consolation for this increase competition for fashion jewelry, this makes your present jewelry even more valuable than ever before!

But did we ask for this competition for fashion jewelry?

Logically, men should not be ashamed to limit their ambitions to earrings and jewelry. We hereby recommend that real he-men purchase from the *Link-Us* website, the following items to successfully complete their feminine wardrobe:

1. *Lipstick.* Take along several colors for the road, so you can mix and match. For example, bring along red and green during the winter months, and yellow and purple during the spring. Orange and black are ideal for October, while something light and relaxing, say chartreuse, is most suitable for the summer.

2. *Panties.* Since men are already exposing their underwear, why not really show women what they're made of? Those in relatively good shape can attempt the thong, G-string, or even crotchless panties, while those in weight reduction programs may be better served

holding out for the Grandma pantalooms. Don't be ashamed to COME OUT and really show the world your love for lingerie.

3. *Matching bra.* Again, we are only *recommending* that the bra and panties match. It's truly up to your imagination, as an American he-male, to decide. Since men have differences in chest structure, you can vary your choices. It's as simple as the alphabet itself: A, B, C, D, and for those really overweight, dare we include the "E" cup? Men who feel somewhat risqué can even go for a push-up bra, of particular help when feeling lonely at the bar and all that's left are other lonely men, looking for someone to cuddle and hold just for the night. Reel those bad boys in!

4. *High Heels.* Another must! We recommend spending a full weekend shopping for all your selections. How do you feel about open toe? Do you prefer low or mid-sized heels? Strapless heels, or those with all sorts of latches and strings? Don't be ashamed to let other men know your *SECRETIVE FEMININE INSTICTS.* It may be a good idea to buy some fashion magazines too, and make sure your overall body theme is in sync.

5. *Wigs.* One of the few opportunities to give bald (or balding) men a chance to really make a difference. Get several choices of style, length, color, you name it. For those who don't get out much, take a chance on a platinum blonde wig! We all know that blondes have more fun, and so will you.

6. *Purse.* What real he-man today should be forced to rely on a flimsy, tiny wallet just because of convention? There are all sorts of things you can carry in your purse: lipstick, perfume, foundation, eye mascara, mace or pepper spray (to ward off overly

aggressive women!), hand tools, clawing hammers, grinders, chippers, grabbers, nail guns—the potential is unlimited here. Don't be ashamed to use your imagination. We know you can do it.

Once successfully completed, the finished he-male wardrobe will be ready for nearly any night out with that special someone. For the woman who doesn't like competition from her date—*BEWARE!*

And if you're considering falling for a guy with an earring, just remember: even a little diamond stud or a tiny gold ring can lead to the bigger, bolder stuff!

ROAD RAGE WHEELER PEELER

The Wheeler Peeler assumes that women are all deficient behind the wheel, as compared to the typical male. As a result, this confused bogus male never feels fully complete unless he is displaying what he thought he learned in Driver's Ed class.

Road Rage Wheeler Peeler is a special category of boys and men who may not even be experienced with any motor vehicle. But even assuming the Wheeler Peeler has received (or kept) his driver's license, the question is, to what extent should the gas pedal be depressed, given the position of the rear bumper of the car just mere inches ahead? From what was learned in physics class, it is questionable whether several seconds of time can be gained by tailgating the innocent driver in front.

Assuming 10 seconds are gained per day, that totals to 3650 seconds per year, or roughly just over an hour per year! Now, with an extra hour per year, there are lots of things the Wheeler Peeler can do. He can head to the liquor store and get a couple of 12-packs on sale. If he has a small front yard, he can cut the grass in time for the next football game on TV. He can also wash his car or truck (depending on elevation, of course).

Yeah, I'm crazy. But just you wait and see how I DRIVE

In all this haste, how comfortable will a woman feel on her date with Wheeler Peeler? Suppose a small child dashes across the road in pursuit of a Frisbee or soccer ball? Suppose someone's dog or cat makes a quick dash to the other side of the street, only to have one of the tires rolled nicely over his legs. Wheeler Peelers don't just have a need for speed, they speed to the next *NEED!!*

What could that next need be?
Beer.
Porn videos.
Chewin tobacco.
Chips n' salsa.
Drive-through cheeseburgers.
Huntin'.
Fishin'.
Drill bits.
Hammers.
Studs.
Drywall.
Vodka.
Whiskey.
Rum.
Scotch.
Red wine.
White wine.
Blush wine.
Gin.
Malt liquor.
Or anything else that will fill the need for that moment!

I only drive STICK

Truth is, Wheeler Peelers don't really need any excuse to take to the road; they only need the pedal to the metal. We learned once that big problems (like road rage) wouldn't have gotten so big had they been handled when they were small.

Eventually, one of the trees will dash in front of Wheeler Peeler and put a nice dent in the front hood. Make sure you're not in the front seat with him!

GIMME ANOTHER BREWSKI
FOR DA ROAD

If rough tough earring-infested, baggy-pant-afflicted, backwards (or sideways) baseball-cap-wearing, speeding drivers in mega-tire pick-up trucks don't set off your early-warning indicators, then we hope that coupling any of that with alcohol will set off every red-blinking siren in your bogus-guy radar. Although much of this book is intended to be humorous, being in the same vehicle with a drunk driver is no laughing matter!

Having witnessed drivers in many a CLOSE CALL, we've learned that accidents only need ONE TIME to happen, and alcohol + driving is a dangerous mix and geometrically increases the odds for a big one.

"GIMME ANOTHER BREWSKI FOR DA ROAD" is as common and casual a request as asking for another cigarette, or a piece of beef jerky while behind the wheel. But your life faces immediate danger with one of these drivers, and while drinking can occur anywhere, public safety is under siege when the lives of the innocent, both inside and outside the vehicle, are in the hands of a drunken driver. You should never be one of them—either the driver, rider or the victim!

Gimme one more Brewski for da ROAD

Most of us can point to a friend or a relative who was killed by a drunk driver. You don't want to be another statistic.

One trouble with alcohol is that it makes the driver feel invincible, and all caution seems to go out with the wind. It's bad enough if an intoxicated driver takes his own life; it's even more tragic when he takes others with him. Tragic—and *preventable*!

Make it as clear as possible: If you are dating any guy who is drinking and driving, please, for your own safety, don't wait until the accident happens. It's up to you to ensure your own well being!

BUT I HAVE A
COLLEGE DEE-GREE

It's been said that *CHARACTER IS WHAT A PER-SON DOES WHEN NO ONE IS LOOKING.* What do you think *YOUR* man does when you are not looking?

Today's college-educated graduate may have the skills to get a job and support a family, but, just as frequently, this is not the case. The early child-rearing years, and even the college years, often fail to produce the inner discipline needed to shift from parent-supported party-college boy to a man of maturity, confidence, vision, motivation, ambition, stability, and humility.

As you start to FINE TUNE your husband search with a prospective mate, check to see how he handles a full range of basic college-educated functions. Does he communicate with you in clear, effective English, so that most people in America could understand what he is trying to say? Can he write a sentence that makes sense? Does he ask questions and listen to your responses? What about remembering what you told him? Does he do what he said he would do?

What about when he's wrong? Perhaps the most difficult thing a man can do is admit to making a mistake or apologize for a hurtful action. And while every one of

It all STARTS with a good EDU – KATION

us will make a mistake now and then, one should learn from that mistake and try to never repeat it.

When it comes to character, we are not particularly impressed with any person's college credentials; rather, what did he choose to learn while in college? And does he continue to ask questions, to read, listen, and learn?

When Chip was growing up, his dad taught medical school at the College of Osteopathic Medicine in Des Moines, Iowa. He would say, "I like to teach my classes by assuming that none of the students know a thing. Once that foundation of ignorance is established, I can then begin to build the blocks of success to get them ahead in life." Although many college students have a good high school academic foundation, college is more than just adding to that foundation. It is about preparing for adult life!

It has been said that the mark of a truly educated person is someone who freely admits *I DON'T KNOW.* And, more important, he or she not only knows where to find the answer, but actually takes the trouble to find the solution. Continuous education and growth also occurs outside the classroom and should cease only with death.

Today's competitive labor force doesn't leave much to chance. While it can be true that "It's not what you know, but who you know," the real test is not how well a person does on the interview; it's how that person performs once he or she is hired. It's great that he got a job; now can he keep it—and progress?

When your next BOYFRIEND explains he has a "college dee-gree," take a closer look to see what sort of person he is on the inside. If he is self-disciplined, has a positive attitude, is willing to ask questions and learn, is refined in manner and approach, is courteous and polite, takes excellent notes, and is both a great listener and communicator—chances are he actually learned something from his college days.

However, if he gives the appearance that he knows it all, *BEWARE!*

OH MOMMA,
WHAT SHOULD I DO?

Cell phones have provided a remarkably versatile addition to the way we communicate. Remember when just having a phone answering machine was amazing? Come home for lunch, check your MESSAGES and take notes to provide follow-up calls later that afternoon or evening.

With the advent of nearly every form of cell phone technology, camera capability, and computer interface imaginable, a new danger has emerged with respect to the American male: the "Oh Momma, what should I do?" syndrome. This syndrome is widespread for the many men who never acquired discipline or wisdom from their dads—if they had dads—and for the most part depended on their mothers as the structural framework in life. Cell phones have now relinked grown men back to childhood days, when all they had to do was cry out to *MOMMA* from the back yard, and Momma would come a'runnin'.

Don't get me wrong. Each of our moms were great. She wouldn't even have to wait for any special signal or call. Anticipating most of our needs before they arose, there would appear fresh-baked brownies,

Oh Momma, I'm out of toilet paper. Help me Momma !

cupcakes, pies, you name it, on ready alert for us. Top it off with some chocolate milk or a cold soda, and things were good in the neighborhood.

As the time came to move on to college, graduate school, the military, corporate career, or other facets of life, our moms were still there in the wings—ready as always to weigh in on the decision-making mix, especially when our challenges involved other women. But only when asked!

Because today's cell phones allow instant and constant connection with Momma, many of today's men never graduate from childhood habits, knowing that regardless of any circumstance, ole Momma is there.

Now, I'm not talking about sharing important events, such as "Mom, I'm getting married," or "I got a great new job," or other fairly important news. Instead, we're talking about the Momma's boy—the man who never really grew up. The little boy on the inside who needs his *Momma* to make everything all right!

If you marry such a man, you may find yourself in heated competition with your new Mother-in-Law. Be aware that she may attempt to control the shots and leverage decades of power into the very privacy of your new marriage. And why shouldn't she act on the habits of a lifetime? For each day, every day, today's immature cell-phone boy will ask Momma a full range of questions, such as:

"Momma, I need to run to the bathroom, is that okay?"

"Momma, I can't decide whether to go with Daphne tonight, or Rachel. Who do you suggest would be the better date?"

You know, I MAY have discovered Victoria

"Momma, my friends want me to go out to the club, but I need to watch the college football playoffs. What should I tell them?"

"Momma, I'm hungry and it's eight o'clock at night. Can I come over for something you can cook for me?"

"Momma, I have some dirty laundry, and would you mind ironing my blue shirt for work tomorrow?"

"Momma, I've gone over my credit card limit and I'm with Sarah having dinner. What should I do?"

"Momma, the frozen TV dinner says I can either microwave or cook at 350 degrees. Which one is better?"

"Momma, the police officer pulled me over for speeding. Can you come over here and fix it for me?"

"Momma, I got into a fight last night at the bar. Will you let me come over and take care of me?"

And our favorite: "Momma, I got Lisa pregnant. What should I do next?"

If you've overheard your boyfriend's endless cycle of daily calls, you might conclude that he secretly wants to marry his MOMMA instead of you. For some women, however, this may fit your idea of a fun future, as they can plan on having plenty of time to do things with their relatives and friends when their husbands are with Momma.

Warning: Pay close attention to "who supports whom!" If he's thirty and still lives with Momma, or if she's the one still paying all the bills—watch out!

WHO YOU CALLIN'
FOUL MOUTH?

Many men have had the opportunity to be raised in or have experienced an all-male environment at some time in their developmental years. Think gym class, athletics, the military. . . .

Male testosterone + male ego can easily produce all sorts of foul language now and then. Not that any form of vulgarity is excusable—but nor is it easily restrained when others slip into its usage.

If you've ever been rear-ended in a car accident, the first words out of your mouth probably were not, "Oh SHUCKS, what do you know, my car was hit from behind." Rather, it comes natural for the average person to shout some form of profanity that, while perhaps never helping in any way, at the time psychologically, it seemed to provide a release of *MENTAL ANGUISH.*

Today's male needs to practice constraint from resorting to this lower form of communication as much as possible. Since many males may encourage this form of communication, they may need help from a considerate female to emphasize that it is not appropriate, nor wanted. If a person is very poorly disciplined before the marriage, what do you think he may be like when you finally tie the knot?

Don't you be callin me no jive TURKEY

Thanksgiving dinner with the In-Laws might go something like this:

Mouth: "You pack a mean, hot @@@@ stuffing."

In-Law: "Why thank you, Mouth."

Mouth: "Git me some more of dem mashed potatoes. Dey are

@@@kin GOO—OOOD!"

In-Law: "Here you go, Mouth."

Mouth: "After all dis pumkpin pie, I'm gonna take one big

@@@T. Is anybody in da BADROOM?"

Chances are that you can multiply that vulgarity by a factor of 10 when the real pressures and responsibilities of a family come into play.

Tony's dad taught him: "A fish doesn't get caught if he keeps his big mouth SHUT." Lesson learned for us all.

For the woman who wants to avoid this kind of male talk, don't tolerate it. You have to be clear and forceful, when it first comes out. If you laugh or ignore it, then you are actually encouraging it.

Remember, the Bogus Man uses vulgarity because he can't think of the appropriate words to say. Accepting gutter talk from your date or future date, puts both of you in the same place!

ONLY BRUSH THE TEETH
YOU WANNA KEEP

Ever buy one of those new high RPM tooth-brushes? Once you get going, it's fun to be fully conditioned to brush (or should we say polish?) teeth each time. But what about those who never pay much attention to tooth-brushing, let alone FLOSSING? After all, teeth seem pretty durable, and besides, in a few hours, time to be eatin' again.

Tooth-brushing is one of the universal requirements for quality men. If your man fails to clean something so tiny or hidden as a rear molar, chances are he has other hygiene issues too. Even rich people have to brush!

Soap, deodorant, shampoo, mouthwash, floss, and a handy toothbrush are signs of self-respect and refinement, and a form of politeness that society used to remember.

If your man isn't comfortable with showering, isn't interested in personal hygiene, let alone chewing his food with his mouth closed, showing manners at the table, opening the door for others, and saying key words like "Please" and "Thank you," *BEWARE!*

Listen up. I'll brush when I'm good and ready, you got dat ?

Brushing teeth after eating prevents all sorts of bacteria from growing in hidden oral recesses. Not only does bacteria cause tooth decay, but it also creates an offensive odor and smell. Imagine kissing that!!

If he doesn't take the time to at least brush his teeth twice or more a day, chances are he won't have to brush his teeth in a few years. They will be replaced with DENTURES.

If a man doesn't take the time to brush his teeth, it's a sign of other poor personal hygiene flaws that mark the bogus man. Just in case he may be unaware, buy him a tooth brush. If he doesn't take the hint, look elsewhere!

WHAT DO YOU MEAN, LISTEN TO THE WOMAN?

Both our dads told us that women are masters of communication. It appears to us that their gifts are not limited to the verbal or even the non-verbal. As an American woman, science has discovered evidence that you have genetically evolved with your ability to manage about 20 things at once and still focus at the task at hand. This means you can simultaneously:

Talk on the phone.
Answer the front door.
Work on your business assignment.
Check the mail.
Make a withdrawal at the bank.
Take the dog to the vet.
Get the car washed.
Get the car detailed.
Shop for this week's grocery supplies.
Check out the latest *VICTORIA 'S SECRET* catalog.
Run to the scale to see if you can wear whatever you ordered from *VICTORIA 'S SECRET.*
Seeing that you can, head to the MALL.
Turn on the news to get latest highlights.

So what you're sayin is, listenin to women is important?

> Complete the work assignment due tomorrow.
> Pick up dog from the vet.
> Check your checking account balance while at the

vet.

> Make a deposit at the bank.
> Order a Venti Mocha from Star BUKs.
> Grab the open parking spot before 3 others.
> Go home and let the dog out.
> Put your feet up and read this book.

Beginning a new project is different for everyone. For the average male, we found that it was easier to start one project at a time, blocking out everything else until it is complete. Although this process seems to make the most sense, we are amazed that most women can easily accomplish all that is necessary for multiple projects, and more, including engaging in necessary and superfluous communication at the same time.

The most difficult thing for men is to not only *hear* what a woman is saying, but to *LISTEN* to the meaning of her conversation—even to anticipate or predict where her next sentence or question may go. We've been told women like that.

Men: Women have taught us to truly listen to what they are saying, and of course remember what they said. In so doing, it shows her that you care about her as a person. If a woman sees that you care about her and her feelings, chances are you will find less time for the sports scores on television, and more time for other types of activities—which also serve to build a mutual trust and love together. It can help develop the type of compassion and romance she is looking for, and hopefully you are too.

Chip's dad always taught him, "Don't think that physical attraction will keep a marriage together. True beauty is not what is on the outside, but how that person of beauty feels on the inside. If you can't start the first day understanding her thoughts and views, and project where she is going in her life, chances are you're bound for divorce, and soon."

Women: Our only addendum here, if we may, would be to ask you to go slowly with most of us guys here, especially since few of us have received the DNA gene pool ability to handle 20 things simultaneously. If you can see that we are trying, maybe that's another chapter of success between men and women in America.

We are always willing to learn, and we appreciate a woman's helpfulness to patiently teach.

In summary, if a man displays the unwillingness to listen to you, nor respect your opinions and expressions, chances are working and living together is beyond this bogus man's capabilities.

"BUT MOM,
HE GO TO CHURCH ON SUNDEE"

Most Americans take their spirituality and sense of religion in a personal way. Some like the more dynamic, such as:

> Jumpin'
> Shoutin'
> Dancin'
> Prancin'
> Yellin'
> Tellin'
> What's he sellin'?

Others, like many of us, prefer a more modest sermon and a couple of traditional hymns before and afterwards. But whatever the style of delivery, it's *Buyer Beware* when it comes to the outwardly religious man. For as always, it's the *inward* qualities that count.

Take the time to ask and discover: What is the church attendee like throughout the rest of the week? A man can display all the right bells and whistles when it comes to *seeming* holy, but in reality may have never really developed his own God-given personality and demeanor. Unless carefully checked, a woman may assume that his devoted church attendance must mean all

Nothin but the best for Sun-Dee

systems are all right; but the true test is how well he has spiritually matured on the inside. Does he apply fundamental ethical and moral values in his dealings with others?

Can it be possible for a person to present an image to others, seeming to say and do everything *RIGHT*, yet not know who he truly is as a person? It seems to us that the façade is easy to establish for the bogus man. Many a man hides his own insecurities and frailties behind a façade of "Johnny B Good."

A woman may insist, "But Mom, he go to church on Sundee!" But that may or may not be solid evidence for any real spiritual conviction. Whether a person claims to be a Christian, or a Jew, or a Muslim, or a Hindu, or any of other religion, chances are only God knows what's going on in the inside.

We contend a truer humility shines forth in how a person treats others throughout the week, rather than in one hour of acting *HOLY* during the weekend service. How a person treats animals is also an indication as to how the person will treat children, or even you and your friends, once the newness has worn off.

Each of us has to account for our own link with God. It may be time to *Link-Us.*

FINDING MISTER RIGHT
CHART DE LA FLOW

ASK YOURSELF:

1. Is he MALE or FEMALE?
   Female?
   Male?
   Can't tell?

2. What does his hat look like?
   He doesn't wear a hat.
   He wears it backwards.
   He wears it sideways.
   He wears it over his ears.
   He wears it normal fashion.

3. What does he drive?
   Pick-up truck, normal tires.
   Pick-up truck, MEGA tires.
   Non-truck, looks nice/clean.

4. What jewelry does he wear?
   He ain't got none.
   Earrings, either ear or both.
   Nose rings, eyebrow ring, etc.
   Neck chain.

ACTION STEPS:

Start again.
Good job, go to # 2
START OVER!

Good! Go to # 3
Bogus alert!
Bogus alert!
Bogus alert!
Okay. Move on to # 3.

Could be okay; hit # 4
Bogus alert!
Good! Hit # 4

Good! Hit # 5
Bogus alert!
Bogus alert!
Take a chance.

College ring.
Tongue ball.
Face covered in metal.

Pawnshop or actual grad?
Kinky. But NO!
What do *you* think?

5. How well does he communicate?
   Only one way?
   Spells and speaks clearly.
   Can't spell, speak, or write.
   Has trouble with English.
   Only with smell.
   Let out a good one.

Bogus alert!
#6 is waitin'.
Buy him crayons.
So much for education.
Stay upwind.
Did you call the EPA?

6. Does he drive intoxicated?
   Yes, almost hit a bridge.
   Open containers in car.

   Never.
   No, but he sure can dance.

Call 911.
Bogus alert! This guy's
serious.
#7 is your next one.
Throw a party.

7. How does he drive?
   Obeys laws and
   rules of the road.
   Only 9 MPH over limit.
   Reckless, abusive,
   aggressive driver

See #8 before it's too
late!
Take a chance.
Why are you still in the
car?

8. Does he have the MOMMA's boy syndrome?
   Yes, and it's quite obvious.

   No. He makes his own
   decisions without MOMMA.
   Momma brushes his teeth.
   Momma tucks him in bed
   Sends MOMMA a card a day.

His Mom is on call
waiting.
Almost there, select # 9.

Call psych ward.
What do *you* think?
Better than going to visit.

9. Is he a religious hypocrite?
    Pretty obvious, yes, and rude.   He needs quiet time.
    Can sing like an ostrich.   Who cares?
    Reads the Bible daily.   Sincere? Take a chance.
    No, he seems pretty normal.   Go to # 10 now.

10. Is he MARRIED?
    Yes.   I knew it. Most good
                                          ones are.
    Yes, but to Ralph.   Gay men are out there.
    No.   What are you waitin for?

ROMANTIC WALKS
ON THE BEACH

Few of us would turn down a romantic walk on the beach. Smelling the fresh ocean breeze, feeling cool, tingling waves soaking our toes over the warm sandy shoreline.... Most singles advertisement pages have some sort of reference to this most relaxing and contented feeling.

I need me a woman to cook me dinner

Maybe it's time for all of us to step away from the anxiety of life. Take a moment to picture thoughts of joy. Which of the following may bring pleasure to your own life?

The innocent smile on a child's face

The feeling of warm sunshine on a deserted beach

The strength of a hug from someone close to you

The secret joy of a first kiss

Spontaneous laughter at something funny

The first slide into a warm bath

The sun's greeting when waking after a great night's sleep

The smell of fresh coffee

The feeling of reaching out and helping others

A puppy's eager greeting at the pet store

Taking road trips to nowhere special, with someone special

The inner strength to allow aggressive people the opportunity to "get ahead," when in reality they will be humbled by your own character

Being thankful for life itself

Freeing oneself from the anxiety of not keeping up with the Joneses, but rather reaching out to help others less fortunate

Remembering the good times of the past

Finding humor in nearly any situation

Being grateful for our US Constitution, where individual rights, as opposed to group rights, are written for each of us to cherish and protect

Honoring your dad and mom, regardless of how well they served as parents

Helping children grow into responsible young adults

Going fishing for the first time and catching a small sunfish

The taste of chocolate cake, still warm from the oven

Kicking off your shoes after a hard day's work

Napping 30 minutes on the couch with no one around

Being part of any team, winning or not

Retreating into solitude when the world gets to be too crazy

Reading a book

Taking a self improvement course

Travel to a distant land and sharing smiles together

Memories while opening family photo albums

Dreaming for the best in life

Having hope

Being trusted

Seeing the display of well-groomed manners and etiquette

Being thankful that God has given us the Way of escape,

for those who seek to understand

Falling in love with someone real, devoted, and true

A quality man will focus more on these things, and less on who he can screw over at work that day, in the parking lot, or on the freeways.

These are some of our thoughts, and we hope sharing at least one of them brings you joy and comfort.

BEWARE: Bogus men care only about their own personal pleasure! A walk on the beach for a bogus man is just that!

JUST WHERE IS THIS EVASIVE
MISTER RIGHT?

Single women need to understand that there are not many Mister Rights available. Many have already been taken, and the few who remain are often dismayed that their fine qualities have not been admired or even recognized by many a passing woman. Too many women are more interested in how a man LOOKS rather than in how a man IS inside. How a man ACTS on the outside is frequently an indicator on how he IS inside.

We guarantee that quality, single *Mister Rights* know exactly what we are talking about; while the *Bogus Men* can't seem to understand any of it!

Mister Rights are trying to set the right conduct each day:

No real "road rage;" a sense of humility, humor, hospitality, and cheerfulness; an attentive listener and great conversationalist; has ambitions and hopes; is reflective, considerate, patient, responsible, trustworthy, and thankful.

These are just some of the qualities of Mister Right. Yet, it seems apparent that many women, and those who truly want to find their own Mister Right, not only settle for Mister Wrong, but seem to expect that they somehow deserve to be treated so contemptuously. And, that makes you, *Miss Wrong*. You deserve to be treated with admiration and respect.

We contend this reality is similar to an exotic car passing by on the street. Those who can recognize the finely developed levels of comfort, safety, and design, and the hand-built quality—forged by perhaps decades of engineering, automotive tests, and road races—need only a second or two to admire such heritage. Could this be why some cars as many as four or five decades old are sold for hundreds of thousands of dollars?

A woman also needs to understand that she is more likely about three or more years more mature than most men her age. As she approaches each new birthday, she is literally miles ahead of nearly any man even remotely close to her age.

Hey Girl... it's time we raise the standard in quality MEN !

We're not sure how this happened, although we're sure you've noticed. Around age 10, girls start to recognize that it's a competitive world, particularly among other girls. We would contend—and our women friends have confirmed—that many women today often try to look and act their best, not to impress any *MAN*, but rather to compete, if you will, among her fellow *WOMEN!*

Shopping malls are a great place to test this observation. Most women in shopping malls look not only fabulous, but it's almost like a beauty pageant. To the casual (male) observer, though, it appears as if women are going there to SHOP.

Not necessarily true. Many women are busily checking out the competition: their hairstyles, shoes, nails, makeup, dresses, jeans, jewelry, wristwatches—and did we mention SHOES?

Men don't really recognize any of this. We go to the mall for a couple of things—like a shirt or a pair of socks—then maybe get something to drink or a snack and just get out. Maybe a lemonade and one of those big pretzels.

Women may have mastered the art of LOOKING GOOD while SHOPPING for clothes, makeup, and shoes. However, it may be necessary for you to learn *HOW TO RECOGNIZE THE MISTER RIGHT* who may have just passed you by.

How do you do this? Simple, really. Most Mister Rights would LOVE for any woman to initiate some form of communication. Maybe only a smile when you pass him by in the mall. Maybe you'll drop something on the floor, hoping he will take action to pick it up. Feeling somewhat adventurous, you might dare say the magic word: "*HELLO.*" Now wouldn't that be a shock?

Imagine a quality Mister Right, minding his own business, walking to a department store to get a pair of underwear (worn on the inside, of course!). And lo and behold, you make eye contact. You find him interesting. You do everything right—a subtle tilt of the head, a nice smile, a casual question, like "Have we met before?" Maybe a compliment: "I like your shirt." Does it really matter?

Of course not. Mister Rights don't bother analyzing the contact. They notice only the woman reaching out and expecting the man to be nice in return. The problem for the woman is the difficulty in determining at initial contact whether he is a Mister Right or a Mister Wrong. But nothing ventured, nothing gained! And now you have this guide to help you sort out the instant mistakes!

Unlike the social or nightclub pressures for the man who is trying to *PICK UP A WOMAN,* the entire scenario is nicely reversed when the woman tries to capitalize on the potential of a single Mister Right only a few feet away. However, by taking action to shake things up in a good way, the woman runs the risk of being identified as either too aggressive or desperate.

Not to worry! The key is the smile, the eye contact, the subtle touch. Then let the man take the lead! If he is single or unattached, he more than likely will take the lead. If he's married or unavailable, he more than likely will not follow up. The difficulty is in determining whether the man taking the lead is actually single or a Bogus Man. There is nothing like a direct question to prevent wasting time: "Why isn't your wife with you?" Be sure you watch his body language when he responds!

For the 21st-century dating ritual, the Mister Rights should never have to try hitting on a woman they like, nor memorize some pick-up line or approach. No need to use manipulative psychology to trick the woman into thinking he is someone that he certainly is not. Men who wish to gravitate up to the next level in the food chain will learn to take corrective steps to transform themselves into the new Mister Rights. Regardless of where a person's been in life, what truly matters is not where they have been, but where they are going.

Remember, great baseball players take lot of swings before they find the right pitch to hit a homerun! The question for 21st-century men is: ARE YOU UP TO THE CHALLENGE? If so—pull up your pants and turn that hat around! Get your temper under control and gain some dignity!

The question for women is: *HOW MANY BOGUS MEN ARE YOU WILLING TO MEET AND TO LIVE WITHOUT?*

If BOGUS MEN see their bogus behaviors won't get them the girl, they'll have no choice but to change their BOGUS WAYS. Changing behavior from a bogus man to a potential Mr. Right adds to the pool of Mr. Rights. As we have been saying all along, it's up to the American Younger Woman to set the standards!!

WOMEN'S BOGUS MEN QUICKIE QUIZ:

JUST HOW BOGUS WAS YOUR LAST DATE?

1. When it comes to dinner, he always _____
   a. Opens the door for me
   b. Never opens the door
   c. Never pays the bill.
   d. Pays the bill, but makes a fuss.
   e. Combo package of 2 or more above
2. Mouthwash _____
   a. Yes, I was surprised.
   b. Uses mouthwash, but rarely
   c. That ain't the only thing that needs washin.
   d. B and C above.
3. His hands _____
   a. Were crusty, dirty, and disgusting.
   b. Were clean, with well groomed nails.
   c. Turned into Mister OCTOPUS
      when no one was looking.

4. Looking back on my life, most of my men were
   a. Excellent and well mannered gentlemen
   b. Trust me, I've seen it all.
   c. PEE EYE GEE   PIGS !

5. When he first kissed me, I noticed _____
   a. His tongue half way down my throat
   b. He acted normal, in fact I could use one now
   c. 4 Billion bacteria waiting to attack
   d. Nothing. I was working on finding a way
      Outta there.

6. When he picked me up for dinner, I _____
   a. Had to climb up 20 rungs just to get to the
      truck's inside cabin
   b. Had to wipe some chewing tobacco from
      the seat
   c. Nice car. Maybe too nice. Maybe a rental?

7. When using the bathroom at his apartment, I
   noticed:
   a. The toilet seat was down where it should be.
   b. The toilet seat was up.
   c. Seat up, with spashy mess all over the place.
   d. No toilet paper.
   e. Any combination of B, C, or D.

8. When we shook hands at first, he _____
   a. Gave the term WET NOODLE new meaning
   b. Crushed my hand into oblivion
   c. Went into the rappy hip-hop mode
   d. Seemed normal, but I still had to be careful.

9. At the restaurant, I was observant to notice _____

   a. His charm and most polite manners.

   b. The way he keep looking down the top of our female server.

   c. The way he looked at all the women except me.

10. One thing I noticed on the date was_____

    a. The boy just kept rambling worthless data.

    b. Had nothing to say. Total loser.

    c. Took interest in me, asked questions, and made excellent eye contact.

    d. This guy was a PLAYER. He knew how to pretend to be cool. But he wasn't.

11. On a maturity scale 1 to 10, my last date _____

    a. Was a perfect 10. Only he had a boyfriend.

    b. Was a perfect 10. Only he was married.

    c. Was a 2. Which is why I'm still single.

12. He kept trying to _____

    a. Intimidate any male within 4 miles.

    b. Run others off the road in his Good Ol' Boy Truck.

    c. Get in my panties.

    d. None of the above.

13. When the cell phone rang during our date, it was ___

    a. A wrong number. Accidents happen.

    b. One of several incoming calls. Probably some other woman he is tryin to score with.

    c. His MOMMA, checking on her boy.

    d. The Military. They informed him he FAILED the vocational aptitude test.

    e. His parole officer. They are coming to get him.

14. When he took me shopping, I noticed _____

   a. He had frequent flier discount at the earring and jewelry store.

   b. He made Liberace look like RAMBO.

   c. Was missing BRA and PANTIES. He had on everything else.

   d. Dressed normal. But who's to say those were HIS clothes?

15. His baseball cap _____

   a. Was given to his younger brother, age 10. He no longer wears baseball caps.

   b. Was so big, it covered his EARS.

   c. Had propensity to be backwards, and later hip-hop sideways on a moment's notice.

   d. Combination of B and C above.

16. He told me he was _____

   a. Special Forces Commando; but I'm not that stupid. He couldn't do a pushup.

   b. SPY for the CIA. Heard that line before too.

   c. OB/GYN specialist. Like he's really gonna have a chance to find out.

   d. A high school graduate. At least he could be honest here. But he was still stupid.

   e. None of the above.

TEST RESULTS!!

HOW DID YOU DO?

Correct answers (with explanation):

1. A. If he can't open the door, it only reflects a closed mind.

2. A. And it doesn't hurt to brush now and then.

3. B. If you got this one right, we've got to hand it to you.

4. A. Sounds like you know what to look for. Want to work for us as an instructor?

5. B. Kissing aptitude is essential as you know.

6. C. Even if it's a rental, his credit card went through.

   Now let's hope it will clear the dinner TAB.

7. A. Sounds like the boy has some manners after all.

8. D. Nothing worse than a wimpy, or otherwise crushing handshake.

9. A. Too bad you couldn't videotape him in his voyeur mode.

10. C. Again, this is rare to find such a great guy.

11. C. Makes most sense. Finding a 10 is not likely.

12. D. Good Ol' Boys and overly JEALOUS behavior is typical in today's MALE thinking.

13. A. But he should still turn off the cell phone on dates.

14. D. But see if you can borrow his VICKIE SECRET card.

15. A. Glad to see he put it to good use.

16. E. Hopefully he was not that stupid.

Scoring:

14 – 16:   Send us your resume, girl.

11 – 13:   You have a good eye for quality.

5 – 10:   We'll schedule a counseling session, are you free this Friday? Or would Saturday be better?

1 – 4:   I can see why they sell alcohol.

SINGLE WOMEN IN AMERICA, UNITE!

As professor of graduate level economics, Tony has come to understand the merits of the principle of *SUPPLY AND DEMAND.* It seems to transcend not only business principles, but also social norms in our great country.

When you think about it, the mating ritual is really a supply and demand issue. Women provide the supply, and men have a demand for that supply. Men will wait in long lines; if necessary they will take out large advertisements in the paper stating "I LOVE YOU," buy cars, rings, candy, chocolate, perfume, you name it, to appeal to that supply. Men would even buy lingerie, if they knew that was the magic ticket.

Wanting to know more about this issue, we ventured into one of those lingerie shops to ask exactly what *WAS* Victoria's secret? (The answer was no surprise: it's what's underneath that counts!)

It was once said, "A man will paint his ears GREEN" if that's what it takes to appeal to a woman. If a man is willing to do something totally outlandish, does it not stand to reason that a woman can take this hidden male energy, unite with other American women, and

RESET THE BAR for a new, higher standard in American single men?

If women got together and agreed, *NO MORE AGGRESSIVE BOGUS BOYS, PERIOD,* chances are the bad boys would start to wonder what seems to be the problem. Once they see women want only to date men of respect, gentlemanly behavior, and confidence, they may be susceptible for a change in behavior.

This leaves the bogus men with a real dilemma. Does the bogus man ignore the woman's new standard of quality in her new Mister Right? Or does he start to reflect on his own life and say to himself, "Maybe it's time I learned to GROW UP"?

Of course, new opinions and thoughts are hard to accept at first. A man has to go back to his bed *alone* and without a date that night and the previous nights, and might ask himself, *WHAT HAPPENS IF I START TO GROW UP?* What will my GUY FRIENDS think of me?

- Will they make fun of me that I am starting to conceal my undershorts and wear a belt?
- Will they realize I am no longer the *Bad Boy* on the freeway, menacing other innocent Americans and foreign visitors?
- Will they condemn me for taking off my ridiculous earrings and nose rings, and starting to look like a real man for a change?
- Will they poke fun at me when I trade my megatire pick-up truck for a reliable sedan that gets good mileage?
- Will they wonder what happened to my oversized baseball cap that I've now thrown into the garbage?

- Will they laugh at me when I start showing manners and courtesy to others, and say things such as PLEASE and THANK YOU?
- Will they mock me for being a *GOODIE-GOODIE* when I'm not as prone to use vulgarity and profanity in everyday conversation?
- Will they wonder where the new smell comes from as I start using mouthwash, toothpaste, soap, and shampoo?
- Will they make fun of my new interest in asking questions, in learning from others, in asking how the other person's day is going, in recalling what is important to others, particularly women?
- Will my friends laugh when I'm not driving drunk, or acting like a raving maniac on the open road?
- Will I be ridiculed for turning down the music volume to hearing-conservative levels, and while I'm at it, starting to listen to some of the more classic forms of music, like Beethoven or Coltrane?

Once the bogus boy breaks this bond with the *other* bogus boys, he is ready to begin a new life of maturity, sensibility, and stability as a grown man. Actually, bogus men are embarrassments to Mr. Rights, even if they are already married!

Yes, we envision that united together, American women can singlehandedly transform our country overnight and reduce the number of bogus men. So, it's up to you, ladies—you can DO IT!

CONCLUSION

No book would be complete without restoring **HOPE** to the single Young American woman. These women are not unlike men, longing for true love, devotion, trust, stability, and even having a family someday. There are millions of women who seek to return America to the husband, wife, children, dog, cat, white picket fence, perhaps house on the ocean, fairytale. Which woman is not ashamed to admit that she doesn't want to settle for a mediocre or childish boy? One who hasn't grown up, and maybe never will. There is no reason for a woman to accept a bogus man's behavior.

Instead, we foresee women talking together and dreaming the valuable dreams of love, romance, and being swept off her feet. We predict that she *wants to be loved* and is not willing to settle for *Mister Wrong*. We contend that she is more satisfied being alone on a Friday night than wasting it with some bogus man at a bar.

For these women, may we offer and extend our personal hopes, dreams, and prayers that you find your own Mister Right!

To conclude this effort, we offer the following suggestions:

1. **Set benchmarks!** Establish a quality Bogus Man threshold line above which any prospective male must cross before even thinking about a first date, let alone follow up dates, with you. Insist on qualities such as communication skill, respectable dress, listening, strong values, ambition, personality, stability, and vision. If there is an odor issue, send him off with a "Hi Gene!" greeting.

2. **Mistakes Happen! Learn from them!** Transfer past dating experiences and lessons learned directly to future relationships. This means never repeating the same mistake a second time. And by now, we trust you won't be trying to tame a backwards-baseball-capped Good Ol' Road Rage boy this weekend. Let the police do their job.

3. **Overcome past obstacles!** Eliminate ex-boyfriend baggage and past worries, anxieties, fears, and frustrations, and replace them with hope, dreams, love, desire, kissing, travel, adventure, and road trips to nowhere special. In fact, that should be your first move—take a road trip this weekend and simply get away. Who knows what new quality male may be right around the corner, waiting to meet you!

4. **Seize opportunities!** Keep a sharp eye (using both would be even better) on virtually every man you meet, and try to focus on his body language, manner of talk, sense of humor, finished style, courtesy, and gentlemanly conduct. This also includes observing men who have none of these qualities, which may be as high as 90% in some areas. If he is self-centered and interested in only his pleasures, dump the Bogus Man immediately!

5. **Develop a positive attitude!** Believe that you are a beautiful woman on the outside, and in particular, an even more beautiful woman on your inside, waiting to be discovered. Boldly begin each new day with a smile and hope that Mister Right may be coming today!

6. **Develop other interests!** Quality men are interested in women who have a range of professional, cultural, and physical interests. They admire women who are involved in advancing their careers at seminars or college. Quality men are also looking to improve their minds at cultural and community events. Likewise, men are also interested in improving their physical well being, through tennis, swimming, golf, jogging, circuit gym training, and sky diving are excellent physical activities that could result in meeting men in similar pursuits.

7. **Network!** Tell other women about *Totally Bogus Men II: Social Guide for Younger American Women.* Spread the word! Unite against Bogus Men! Isn't it time you find your own Mister Right?

May God Bless America!

BOGUS MEN CATALOG

We suspect that today's single younger American woman will not be able to make a statement of resistance to Bogus Men without possessing a few of the many *Bogus Men* products. Manufactured with the highest quality, unmatched in durability and reliability, BM® ensures a full 2-year warranty on our products. Optional lifetime warranty: add $ 49.95 where appropriate. Become a BOGUS MEN CLUB VIP member today and receive an additional 15% off suggested manufacturing price on all BM® products.

1. **The BM® Jacket.**
Designed to protect a woman under the most brutal conditions, like walking alone at night in a depressing, gloomy, gang-infested alley or street. Resilient under the most extreme all-weather conditions. Doubles as a woman's multi-purpose vest!

The BM® Jacket comes in *ALL SIZES.* Even women participating in the *Janny Crague* LIPOsuction program, the most advanced system of its kind, will be proud to wear this slimming garment. Includes full KEVLAR lining. Features the specially patented BORNE HIDDEN-IDENTITY® satellite surveillance system, so even Grandma knows when you're refreshing yourself at the women's lavatory. Bullet proof. Grenade proof. Protects against Biological or Chemical warfare attack. Plenty of pockets—we're not even sure ourselves how deep some of them go.

Comes in jungle GREEN, midnight BLACK, and SIDEWALK GREY, suitable for wherever your next travel takes you. Be the first in your neighborhood to wear the BM jacket!

Only $149.95.   Shipping extra. Includes emergency flashlight (batteries included). Sizes: 0 to Rozeann Barr.

BM catalog item number 112300.

Order the optional MATCHING HELMET for an even greater fashion statement! BM catalog item number 112300-H.

2. **BM® Night Vision Goggles.**

Ladies, this is the latest fashion accessory, straight from IRAQUE. Makes even professional stalkers look like pansies. BM Goggles offer special magnification lenses of 10X, giving virtually tenfold increase in zoom lens capability under the blackest, darkest, nastiest, zero light conditions. Be able to spot your ex-boyfriend at an incredible 10-mile range before he gets anywhere near your house or apartment! Thermal scan and infrared capability provide the greatest degrees of reconnaissance. Lightweight and fully waterproof. Black color only. One size fits all.

Special 3-year full manufacturer's warranty. $129.95.

Express shipping: $24.95. BM catalog item number 112301.

3. **BM® INVISIBLE Paint**

You heard it right! Invisible, as in, *YOU CAN'T SEE IT!!!*

BM® searched the world over for the best chemical formula. You'll find many look-alikes, but there's only one original: BM! With this paint, ladies, you can literally block out your car, your apartment, your house, your workplace, or any other location to keep bogus men from bothering you. Now he won't be able to see where you live or work, or see your car going down the highway, so he really can't come after you.

Helps with all sorts of administrative chores around the house, too! Make all your credit card bills *DISAPPEAR!* See a low grade on an old high school or college transcript you don't like? Just paint it over and make that eyesore go away forever!

Mister Right coming over for dinner unannounced? No time for a clean-up? Brush on some BM® Invisible Paint and watch all that mess vanish before your eyes!

Or how about this? Brush some on your ex-boyfriend or ex-husband and . . . presto! Gone for good! He'll never know what hit him.

Unlimited possibilities! Comes in quart-size bottle for monthly applications. Family pack (4 gallons) should carry you through the year.

BM® Invisible paint, quart size: $79.95 BM catalog item number 112302-Q.

BM® Invisible paint, family size (4 gallons): $399.00   BM catalog item number 112302-4G.

4. **BM® JAYMES BONDO CAR**

You've seen the movies and no doubt dreamed of having a car like that! Think it's only a dream? Not anymore! BM comes through again with the world's first BM® JAYMES BONDO car. Runs on solar power, includes jet propulsion capability (for fast getaways), and it uses the LOCKHEAD MARTUN LM 3500 horsepower jet engine, giving you zero-to-60 capability in under 2 seconds. Top speed: (classified). We could tell you, but are you ever really going to go that fast? Let's just say it's over 300 mph.

All sorts of automatic weaponry included, from cross-drilled liquid mercury 5.56 mm, to a 7.62 mm machine gun. Even comes equipped with 120mm titanium-tip rocket launchers! Can easily be converted to White Phosphorous (WP) illumination for night time operations. Optional nuclear warheads are available for the really serious BAD BOYS. (Check with USA State Department before using this feature.)

All-wheel drive is standard. Bullet proof. Rocket proof. Mortar proof. And, Mine Resistant

The BM® JAYMES BONDO car renders highway patrol radar obsolete. Got a tailgater? No problem! Our BM® releasable spike strips guarantee a clean 4-tire blowout in less than 3 seconds. Plenty of creature comforts, including kitchenette, dishwasher, fridge, and microwave.

Also included: a 12-track CD player, DVD player, DOLE-BEE SURROUND system, NAPAS leather bucket seats, power windows, and extra-power brakes.

Comes in either Iridium SILVER or Gothic BLACK.

Total Price for the BM® JAYMES BONDO CAR: $1.6 Million dollars. BM catalog item number 112303.

Optional Nuclear package: $895 Million. (Purchaser must also pass background check.) BM catalog item number 112303-N.

Both models come with 4-week training course, safety certification, weapon certification, FEMAS and HOMELANDISH SECURITY registration and license. Must have clean DMV record last 2 years, including no DUI's! USA citizens only. Sorry, no out of country deliveries. At these prices, shipping *IS* included. We'll bring this baby right to your door. (Allow an extra 6-week delivery for nuclear modification.)

5. **BM® Interplanetary ORBIT KITE.**

You've heard of Men on the Moon. Space travel. Trips to MARS. But that ain't nothing compared to the new BM® Interplanetary ORBIT Kite! Integrating the patented BM® *ANTIGRAVITY* fabric and technology, this kite tells **gravity** to *GO take a hike!* Comes with cushioned 6-foot plus cot with pillow, titanium straps, and locks. Just strap your ex-boyfriend on one of these babies and off he'll soar!

Heard of time travel? Well, that's all he'll have to think about on his way to *PLUTO.* Out of sight, out of mind! Once he leaves EARTH, that's one small step for a man, one BIG step for womankind!

BM® Interplanetary ORBIT kite: $88,995.00

BM catalog number 112304. Shipping included. Specify color.

Comes in Bye Bye Blue, Get Lost Green, or Go-away Gray.

Environmentally safe. Meets OSHAT requirements.

6. **BM® TRUNK WEIGHT**

Many times, Bad Boys just can't take NO for an answer. BM has come up with another INGENIOUS product to really slow him down: the BM® TRUNK WEIGHT! Perfect for his trunk or flatbed pick-up truck, this 8,000-lb. ANVIL will make his little engine work overtime, burning out gaskets, fuel systems, and all sorts of dashboard goodies reflecting the latest computerized engine management technology featured on his truck or car.

Comes with BM® hydraulic hoist to help you ease it into his vehicle, featuring the patented, easy BM® finger-touch design, allowing you to plant a BM® TRUNK WEIGHT even in the wee hours of the morning.

Want extra weight? Go for the MEGA BM® WEIGHT. Coming in at an astounding 19,000 lbs., this is our ***Heaviest.*** We don't care how much horsepower his Bad Boy truck carries, or about his cute little nitrous oxide canister. That don't mean @@@T. In fact, once you install the MEGA BM®, he AIN'T GITTIN' AWAY.

We GUARANTEE to either fully stop, or slow down your bad boy to UNDER 2 MPH, or your money gladly refunded. Bad boys are getting smarter these days, but no worry. This will stop them all.

BM® Trunk weight: $15,999.95   BM catalog number 112305.

MEGA BM®: $39,000.00   BM catalog number 112305-M.

Shipping is free; we have special connections with the railroad system.

Specify color: Turquoise, Pink, Mella Yellow, or Pastel Peach.

Catalog Additions and Recommendations

If any of you readers has suggestions or requests for items that are not included in our catalog, please email them to our website. Our research department will make every effort to analyze marketability and perhaps add the item to our website catalog.

ABOUT THE AUTHORS

Chip Gregory Alan Bunce vividly remembers the cold morning chill of walking over a mile each day to Theodore Roosevelt High School in Des Moines, Iowa, where he spent most of his childhood. From there, he learned how to march as a cadet at The Citadel in Charleston, South Carolina. Finding he had a knack for military life, Chip served in the Army National Guard and the US Navy, where he completed over 20 years of military service to his country.

While in the military, he earned the Navy (and Army) Achievement Medals, Army Commendation Medals, and the Meritorious Service Medal. His positions in the US Navy included Commander of a Combat Craft Unit, Panama Canal; Navigator; and Company Commander of the Naval Mobile Construction Battalion 40. He completed Surface Warfare Officer School in Coronado, California, and Survival, Evasion, Resistance and Escape (SERE) and Jungle Warfare School conducted through US Army 3/7 Special Forces at Fort Sherman, Panama.

In addition to earning his MBA degree in 2001, Chip has finished the Maui Marathon, won a public speaking contest, and traveled the world. He authored his first humor book for women, *Totally Bogus Men: A Social Guide for the American Woman* in 1996. This sequel is a response to popular demand.

Tony Lolas says "Hey from Columbia, South Carolina! I provide the *intellectual side* of our dynamic duo writing team with Chip on the *creative side.* Like Chip, I have been fortunate to have experienced a bit of military service myself. I enlisted in the Air Force to get my "education" and "see the world." Fortunately, I found myself graduating from the USAF Academy with a BS degree in Engineering Management and Economics. Since I figured flying may be one way to travel and see the world, I eventually ended up retiring from the Air Force as a Special Operations Command Pilot at the Presidential level. Must have operated in at least 70 countries; and don't ask me how to spell all the cities I've been able to visit!

Because teaching also seemed to be of interest, I was fortunate to have been able to earn an MBA from UCLA in Operations Analysis, an EdS in Administration and Supervision from Troy State University, an EdD (a/b dissertation) in Computer Aided Instruction and Design from the University of South Carolina (the East Coast USC), and a Ph.D. in Leadership and Supervision with a cognate in Information Systems Management from the University of South Carolina. Since I have always considered myself a bit of an educator, especially with my "BS" degree, I have been privileged to serve as faculty at The Citadel, the College of Charleston, Webster University, and Clafin University. I also teach in the Walden University Ph.D. Information Systems Management program.

In my second career, I was selected as Chief of the Bureau of Business Management for the South Carolina Department of Health and Environmental Control, expanded across the State with 6000 employees in 130 plus offices.

In both these careers, I've been grateful to appreciate and listen to an ever expanding list of *true stories* and *not so tall* tales, where many women share experiences as they search for Mister Right. Not all women were that successful! And, in sampling some of the more interesting highlights, Chip and I have compiled a series of guidelines for Younger American Women to enjoy... *Totally Bogus Men II.*

By the way, any reference to a specific male is purely coincidental. Likewise, any male who may see himself in this book, don't blame us as we only used what we were told by an anonymous female!

Thank you for allowing us to contribute to your hopes and dreams of finding the right man to share your life, by identifying and conforming Bogus Men!

AUTHORS' NOTE

Thanks to all of you who purchased this book. As we are in the process of developing *Totally Bogus Men III: A Social Guide for Almost as Young American Women,* we are open to any suggestions for labels, stereotypes, and experiences that might be of interest to the over forty women who are in this category, or might someday be in this category.

Please don't hesitate to contact us at website address: www.Link-Us1.com, and take a look at other Link-Us products, clothing line, accessories and a future DVD/video.